A BOOK OF

Dragons & Monsters

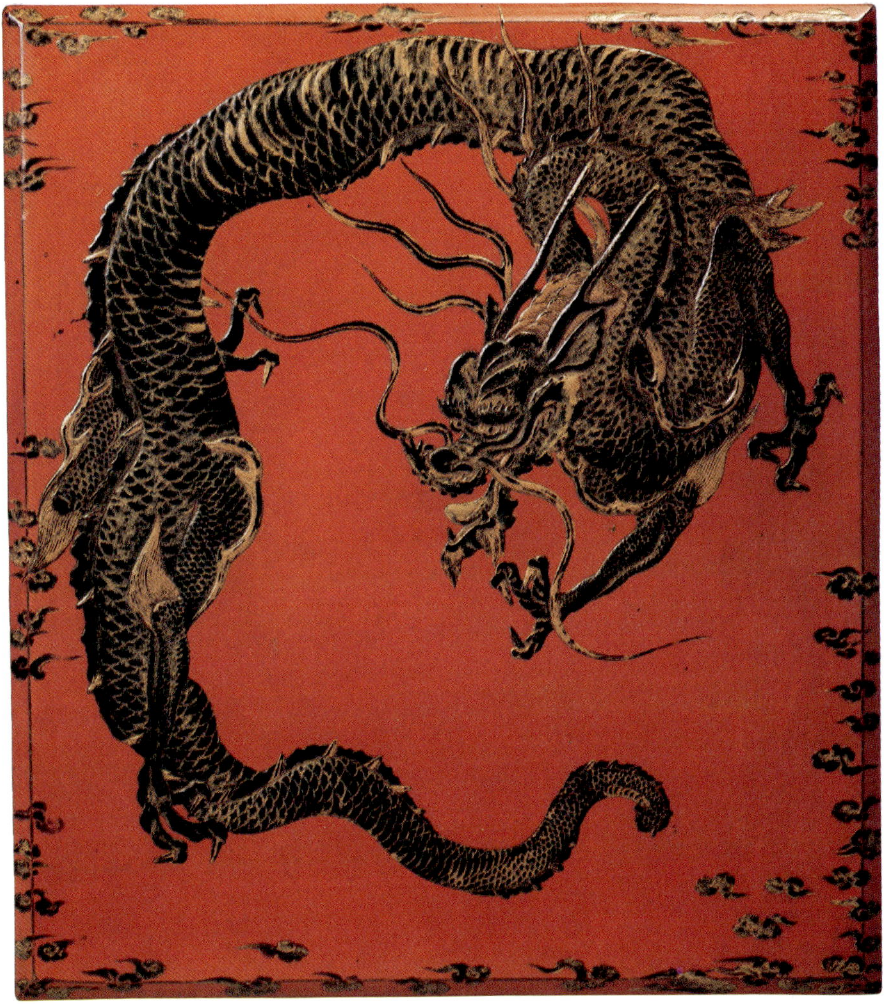

A BOOK OF

Dragons & Monsters

INTRODUCTION BY SUSAN STRONGE

CANOPY BOOKS
A division of Abbeville Press, Inc.
NEW YORK

INTRODUCTION

SUSAN STRONGE

Fantastic creatures have been used to populate myths and legends, and in creating catastrophe or good fortune they explain phenomena that are otherwise terrifyingly random.

Some beasts, such as the dragon, are almost universal, always recognisable even though their significance and representation vary. In the East, dragons, such as the one seen on a Chinese blue and white bottle of the 14th century, are usually very sinuous. There is a strong sense of movement, with flames darting out from its elongated body which is pulled in different directions. A Japanese dragon can be seen on a lacquer box dated 1626. Its black and gold body twists round against a dramatically contrasted brilliant red ground, with Chinese clouds scudding round the edges of the cover. On an 18th century ivory netsuke the dragon curls round a dead tree and clasps a sword in its tail and a jewel in its front claw – two of the three imperial regalia of Japan.

Western dragons tend to be more static and terrible. In the 16th century, the Italian Severo Calzetta da Ravenna stressed the

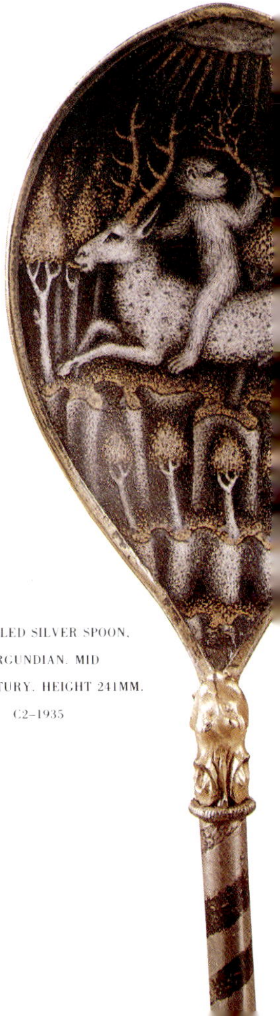

ENAMELLED SILVER SPOON, BURGUNDIAN, MID 15TH CENTURY. HEIGHT 241MM. C2–1935

scaliness of the monster's body, its snarling mouth and terrifying gaze to produce a stunted, grotesque image in bronze. The key elements of scaliness, long serpentine body, pointed tail and muzzle were all that were needed by the unknown designer of the French door knocker of the 15th or 16th century to suggest the idea of a dragon.

In legend, the serpent-like dragon was generally associated with evil and in Christianity came to symbolise sin and paganism, usually being depicted prostrate before saints and martyrs. The slaying of the dragon by St George was ubiquitous in European art and is seen here on the Italian 15th century slate panel.

The Perseus myth provided another opportunity for vanquishing mythical beasts of evil disposition. It may be seen on an Italian maiolica plate of c. 1520. Andromeda, depicted as a rather hefty maiden who seems hardly threatened by the pet-like sea monster, is rescued by Perseus flying in dramatically on billowing white clouds.

PORTION OF A SILK MASKERS COSTUME, TIBETAN, 19TH CENTURY. LENGTH 620–226MM. 18499–1905

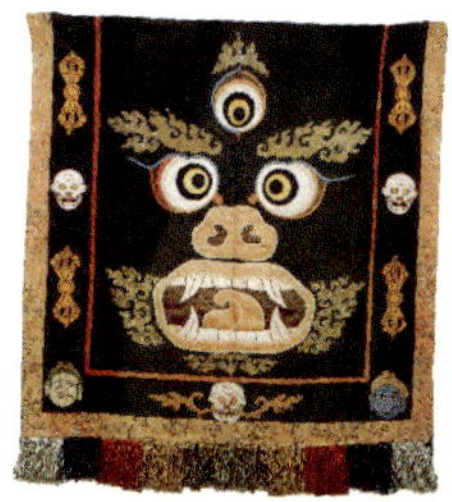

Fantastic creatures were often appealing, even when tinged with ambiguity. The Chinese lion which was known in Japan from the 17th century may symbolise power, but may also be depicted as a puppyish creature with bushy eyebrows who frolicks amongst peonies and tries, without really succeeding, to look fierce. The hatching Japanese *tengu* has equal charm: two ivory netsuke show it first peeping out of a newly-broken egg and then emerging as a slightly confused little beast with a glaring expression. These were mythical forest dwellers with wings and small beaks who were famous for having taught the martial arts to the legendary hero Yoshitsune. Their foe is seen on the print by Utagawa Yoshitsuya (1822–66) where a group of warriors is shown cowering away from a huge angry beast. The hero Minamoto Yorimitsu is accompanied by four retainers who finally slay the giant ogre, Shutendoji, at his mountain lair from where he had been descending to terrorise the neighbourhood.

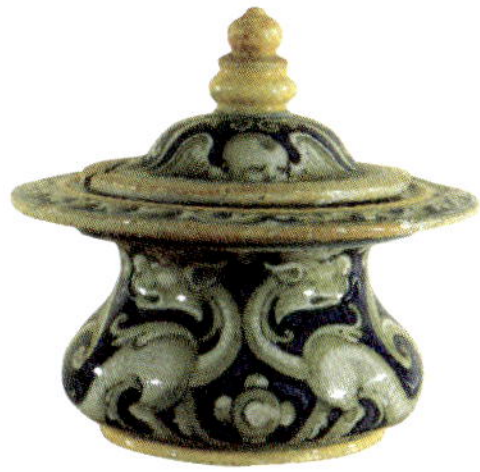

MAIOLICA SALT CELLAR, *C.* 1530.
HEIGHT 160MM. C7142–1861

The significance of fanciful creatures can be lost in time.

Modern eyes are tantalised by the famous Monkey spoon, whose silver bowl depicts, in painted enamel, a monkey sitting astride a fleeing spotted stag, staring back over his shoulder at whatever is behind. The atmosphere of mystery is heightened by the use of a dark greyish-black ground against which the animals appear as ghostly figures, surrounded by trees with pale trunks and foliage like the silvery-gold flames of candles. The spoon is thought to have been made in Flanders for the Burgundian court in the early 15th century.

Medieval metalwork produced ewers with mythical animal masks at spout and handle, a concept also used in the East. A Tibetan ewer of the 17th or 18th century elaborates the masks into stylised bizarre animals, but is designed with a cool restraint reflecting the almost flawless crystal of the body. William Burges, in 1865–6, borrowed the same notion, with very different results, to design the handles of his ewer. Freeing his imagination, he included fanciful architectural features, flowers and other details to the silver gilt mounts.

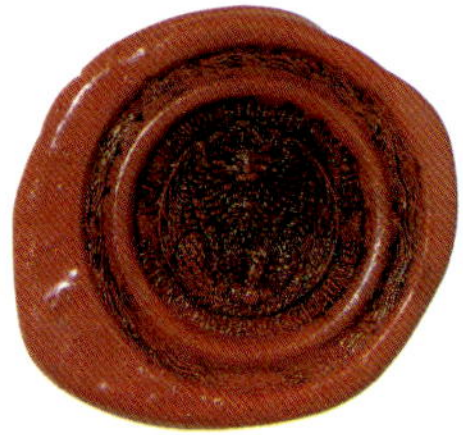

SEAL OF THE BOARD OF TRUSTEES OF THE VICTORIA & ALBERT MUSEUM. BLUED STEEL, SILVER AND GOLD. SCOTTISH. MADE BY MALCOLM APPLEBY, 1985. DIAMETER 110MM. M27–1985

In 1985, Malcolm Appleby produced a whimsical design for a seal for the Board of Trustees of the V & A. He explains it shows a 'thundering great big pussy cat with wings' and was based on sketches of his own cat, John. The cat imperiously stares out, encircled by its wings and with a mane suggesting stylised flames. The fantasy continues with the cat inlaid in gold onto blued steel and surrounded by swirling clouds in different coloured gold inlays. In the best tradition of the portrayal of beasts and monsters, it evokes the supernatural world where anything becomes possible.

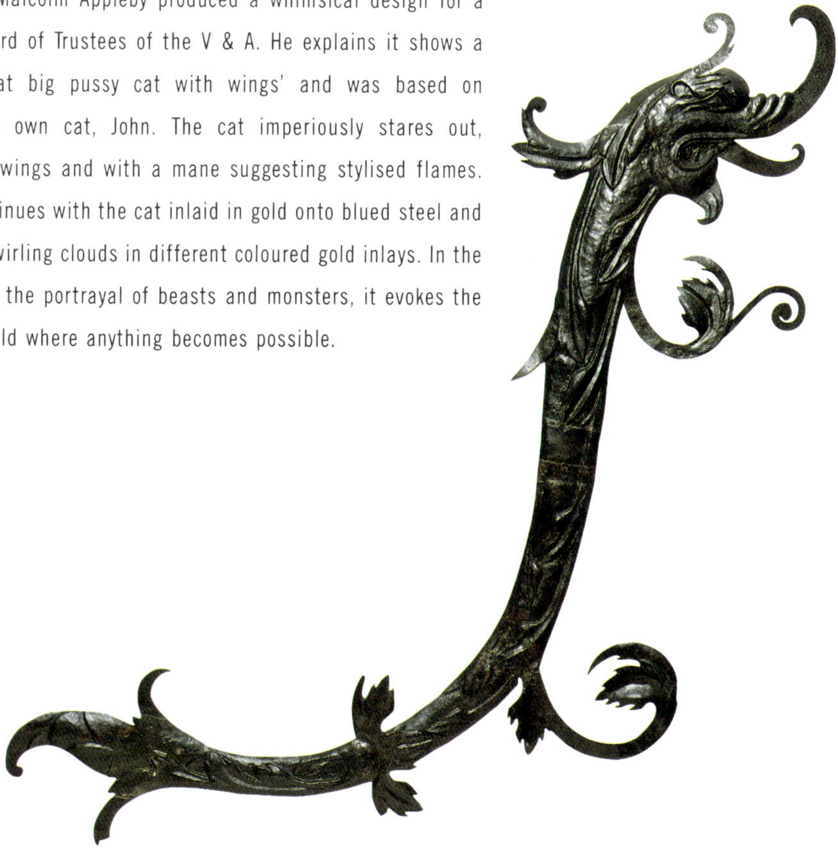

BRONZE DRAGON BY SEVERO
CALZETTA DA RAVENNA.
ITALIAN, MADE IN PADUA,
ABOUT 1500. LENGTH 232MM.
A15–1967

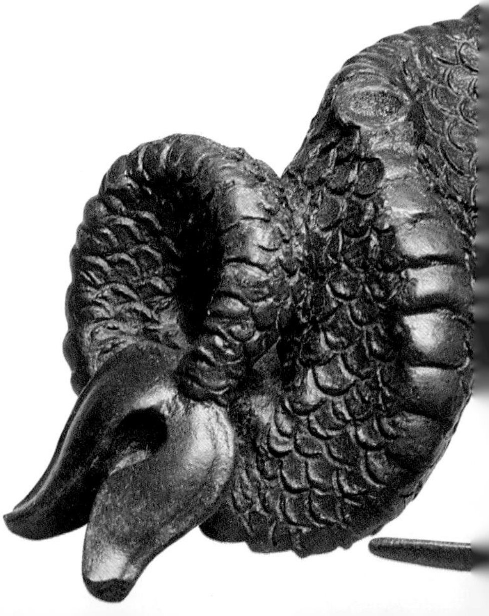

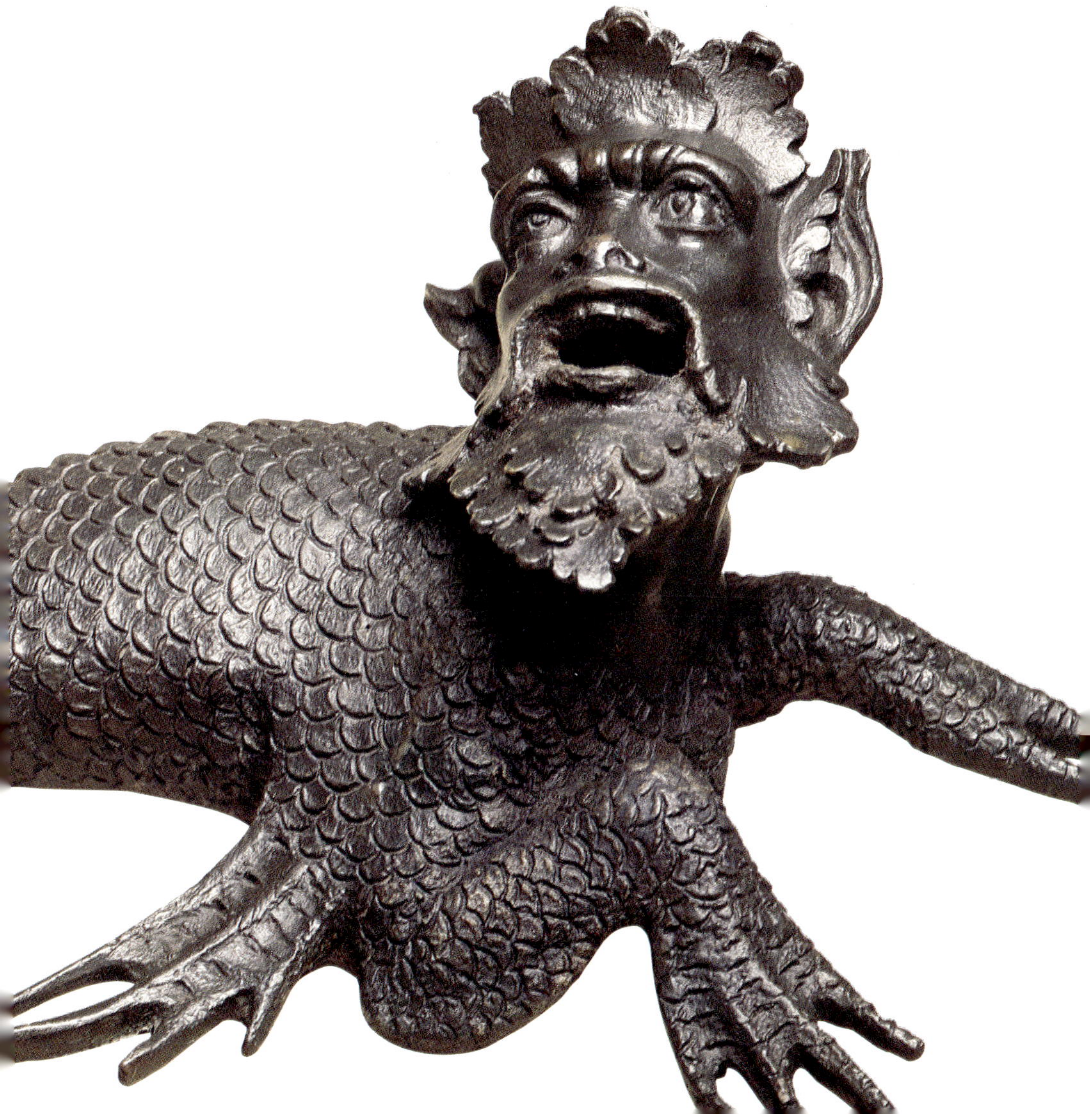

PILGRIM BOTTLE

OF PORCELAIN, PAINTED IN

UNDERGLAZE BLUE.

CHINESE, 14TH CENTURY.

HEIGHT 362MM. C47–1935

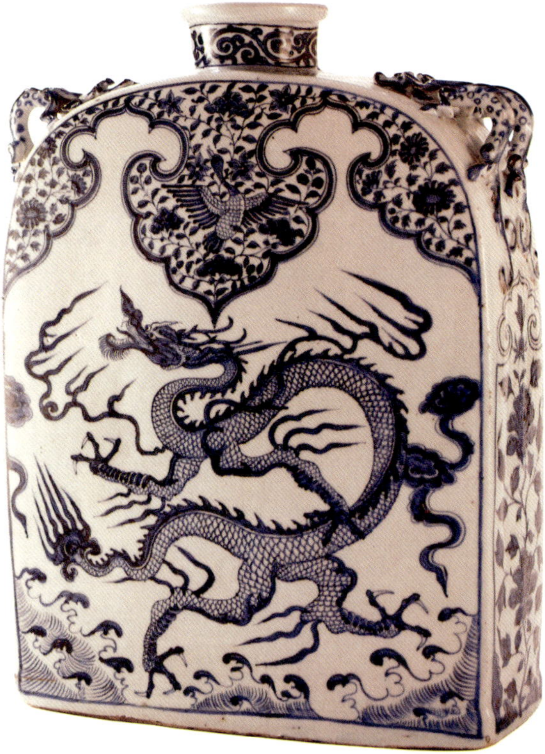

EARTHENWARE DISH

WITH LUSTRE

DECORATION. MADE IN

VALENCIA, SPAIN, IN

THE MID 15TH CENTURY.

DIAMETER 432MM.

C489–1864

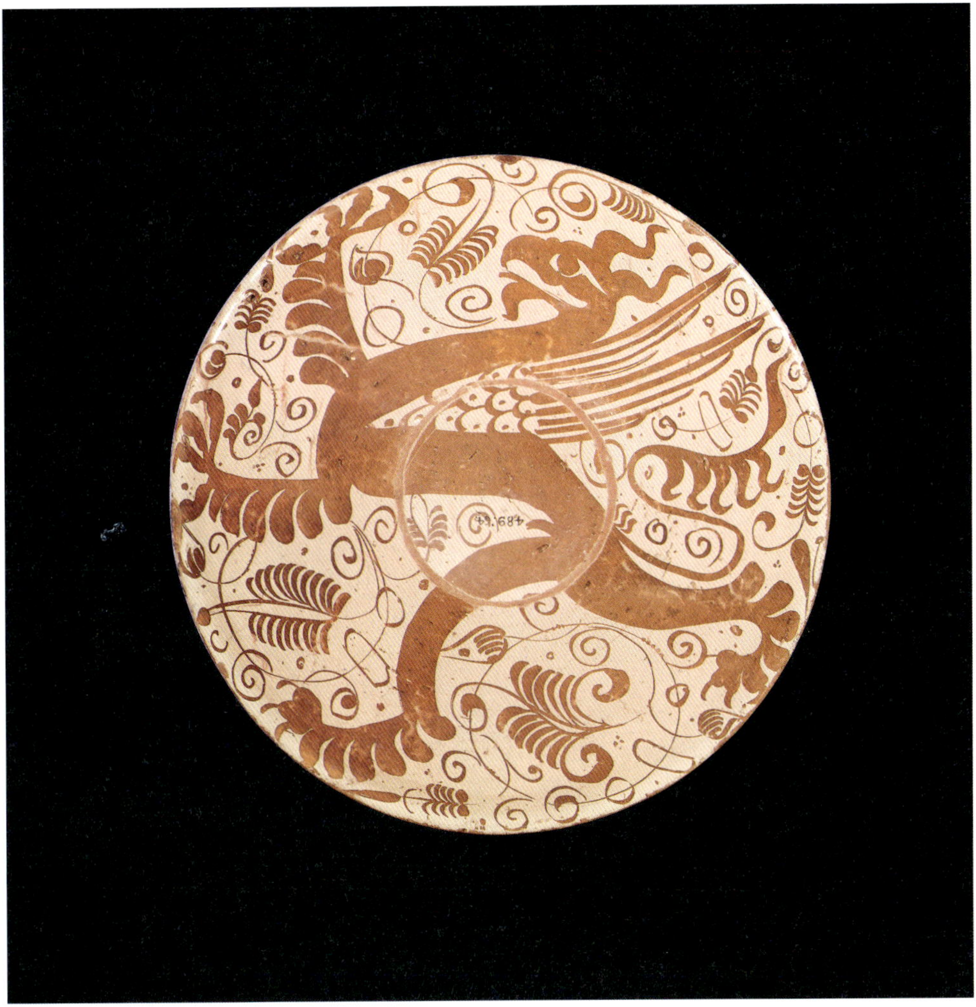

EWER IN THE FORM OF

A CHIMERA. MOSAN, MID 12TH

CENTURY. HEIGHT 187MM.

M1471–1870

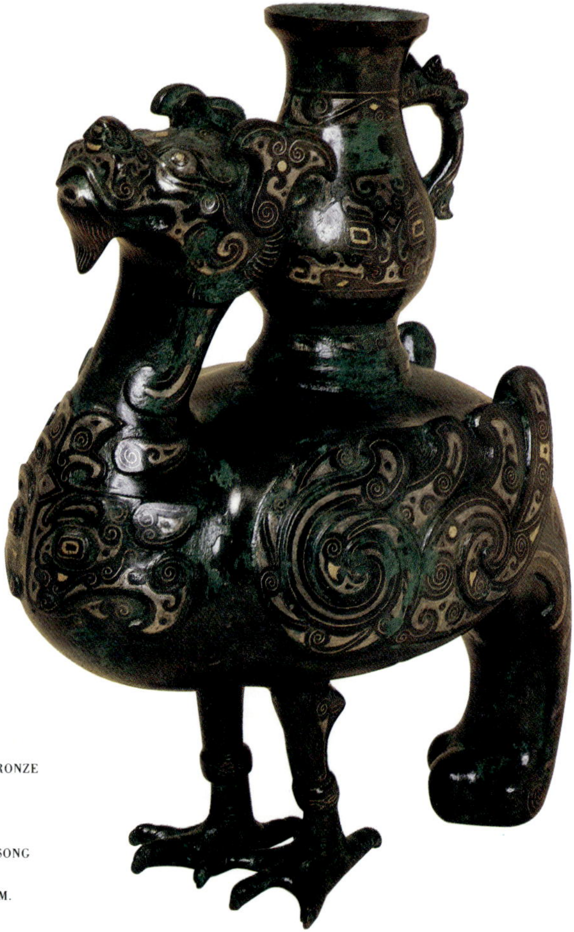

WINE VESSEL IN THE

FORM OF A PHOENIX. BRONZE

INLAID WITH GOLD

AND SILVER. CHINESE, SONG

DYNASTY. HEIGHT 295MM.

M306–1910

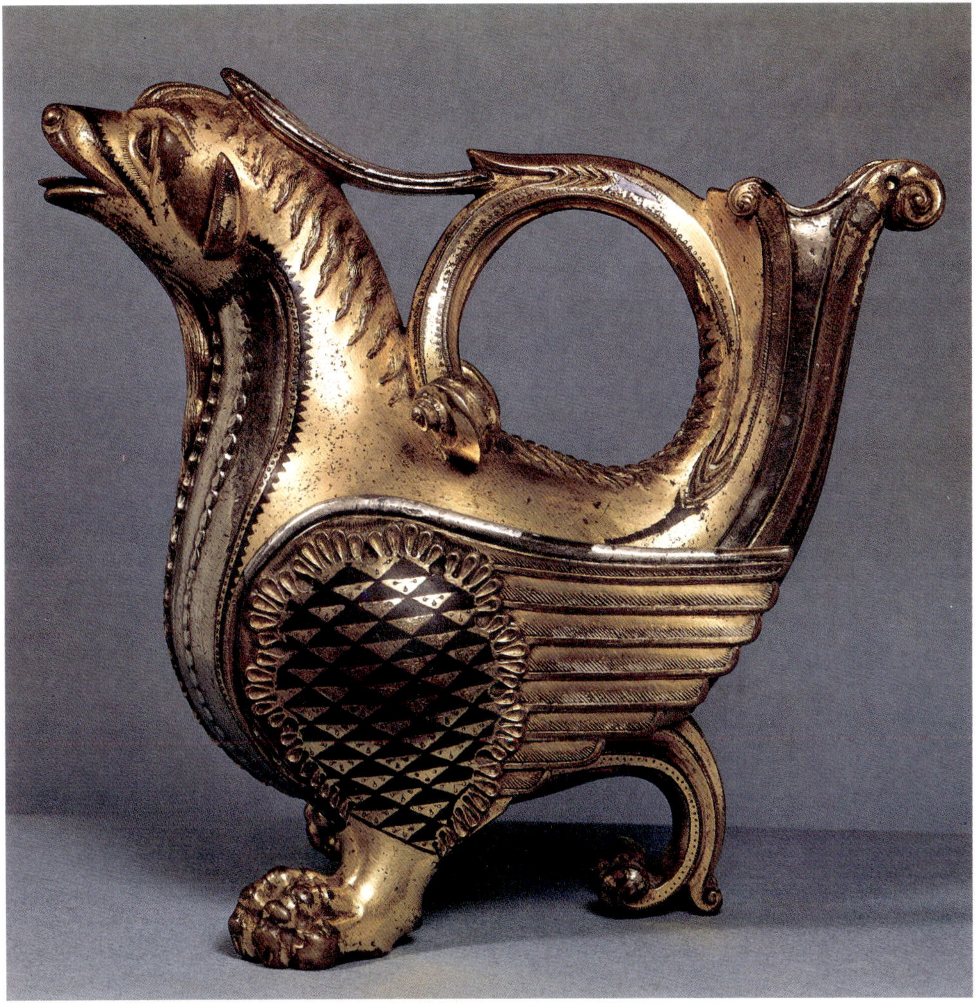

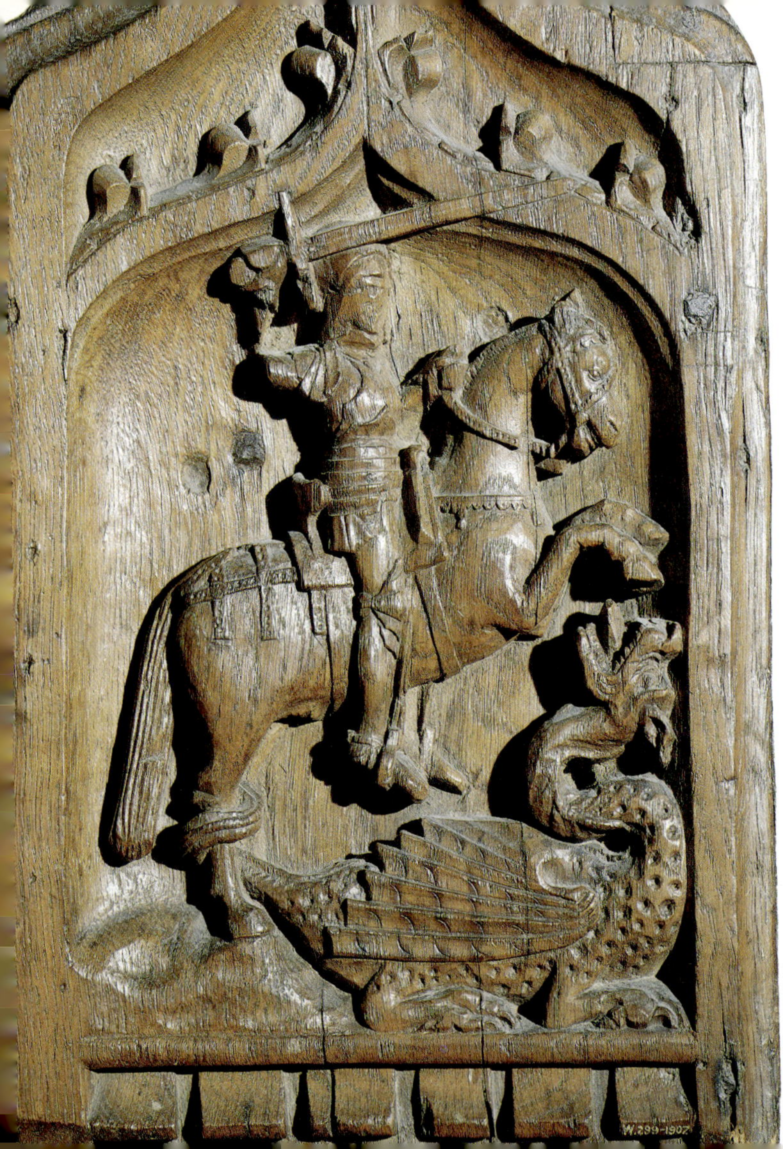

UPPER PORTION OF AN OAK STALL-END. ENGLISH, 15TH CENTURY. 515×270MM. W299–1907

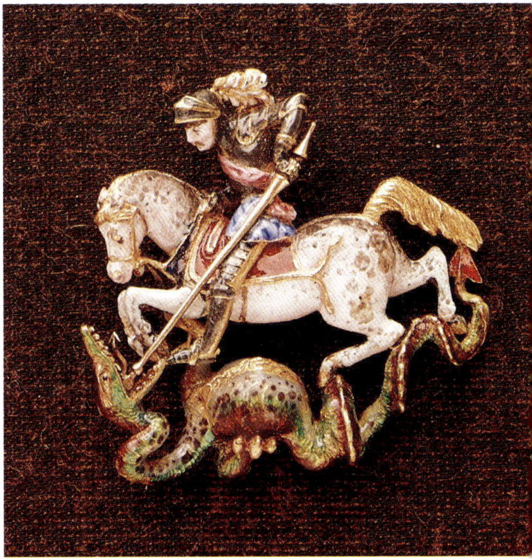

ENAMELLED GOLD PIN,

FRENCH (PARIS), 1855.

LENGTH 104MM.

M2660–1856

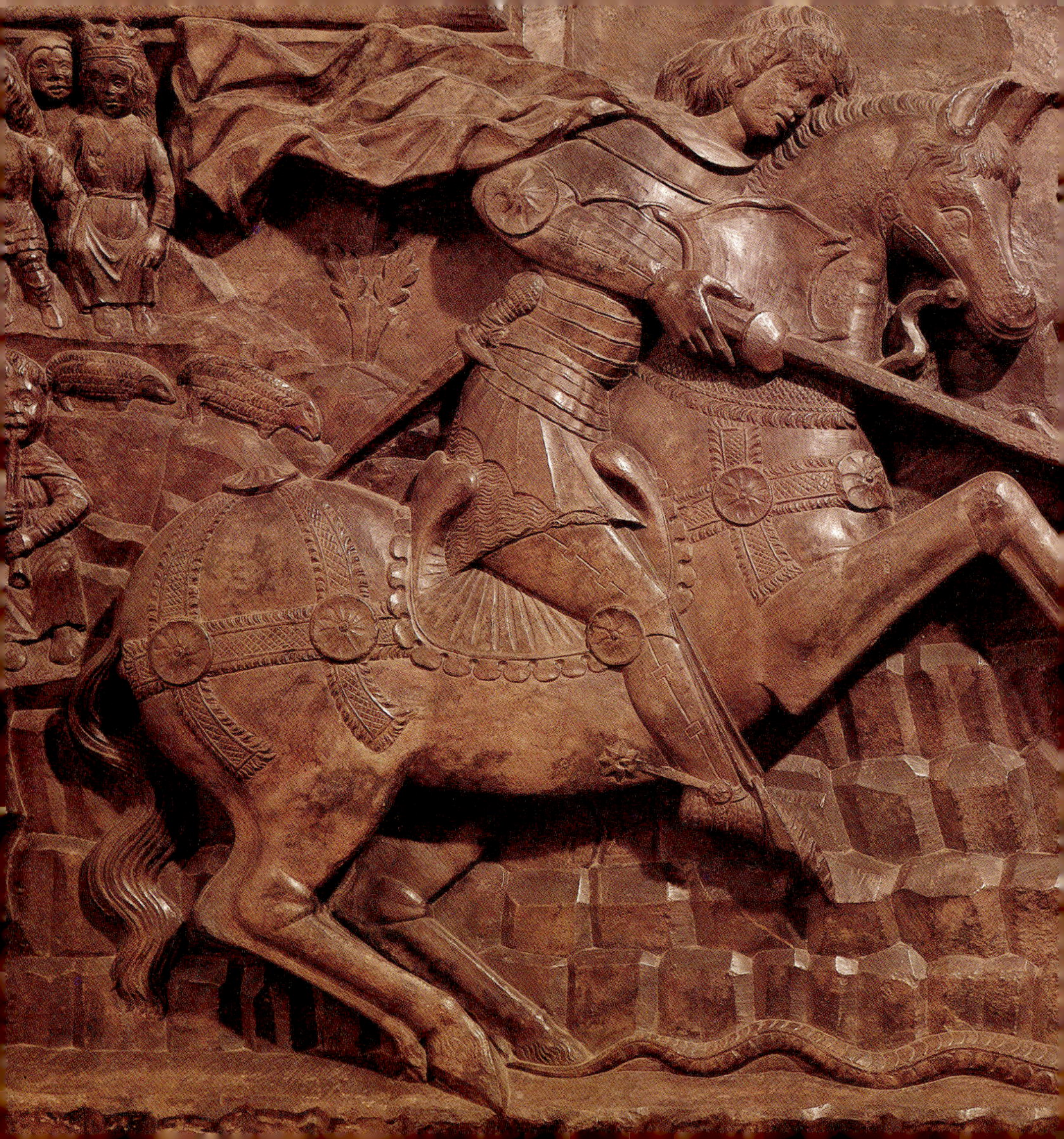

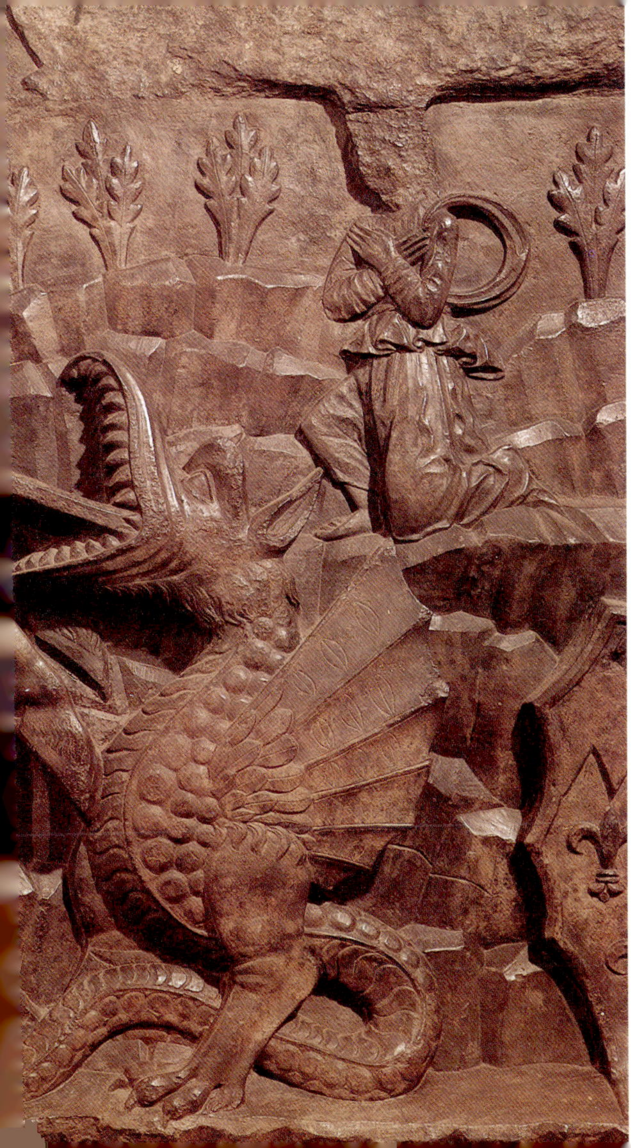

ST GEORGE AND THE DRAGON,

CARVED IN RELIEF

ON SLATE. ITALIAN, GENOA,

SECOND HALF OF THE

15TH CENTURY. WIDTH 1079MM.

A7256–1859

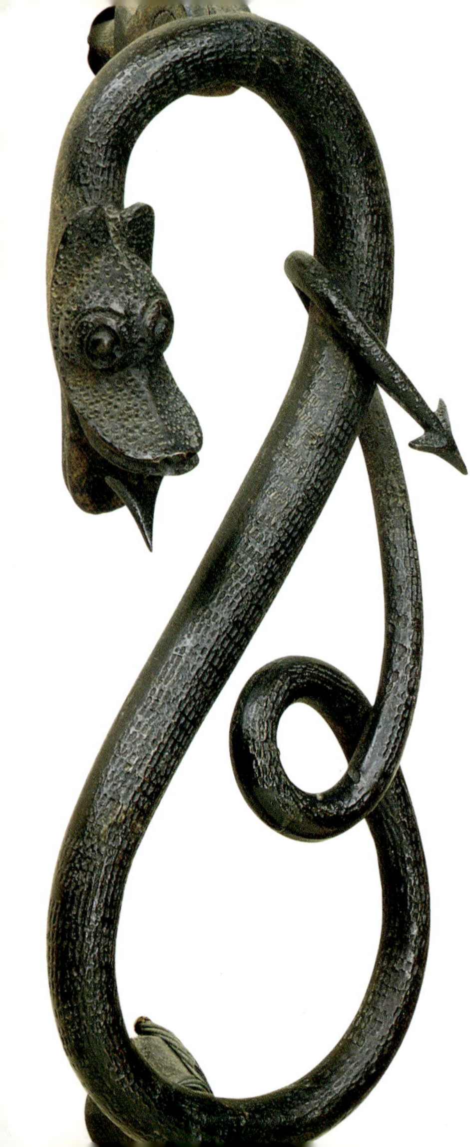

WROUGHT IRON

HANDLE. FRENCH, FROM NEAR

FONTAINBLEAU. 15TH–

16TH CENTURY. HEIGHT 140MM.

M12–1889

PAIR OF CARVED

IVORY DRAGONS FIGHTING

FOR A CRYSTAL BALL.

JAPANESE. HEIGHT 170MM.

1890–1910. A178–1969

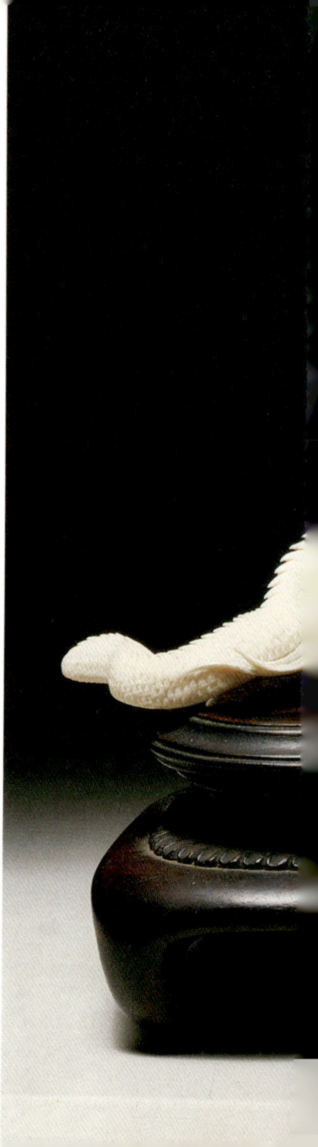

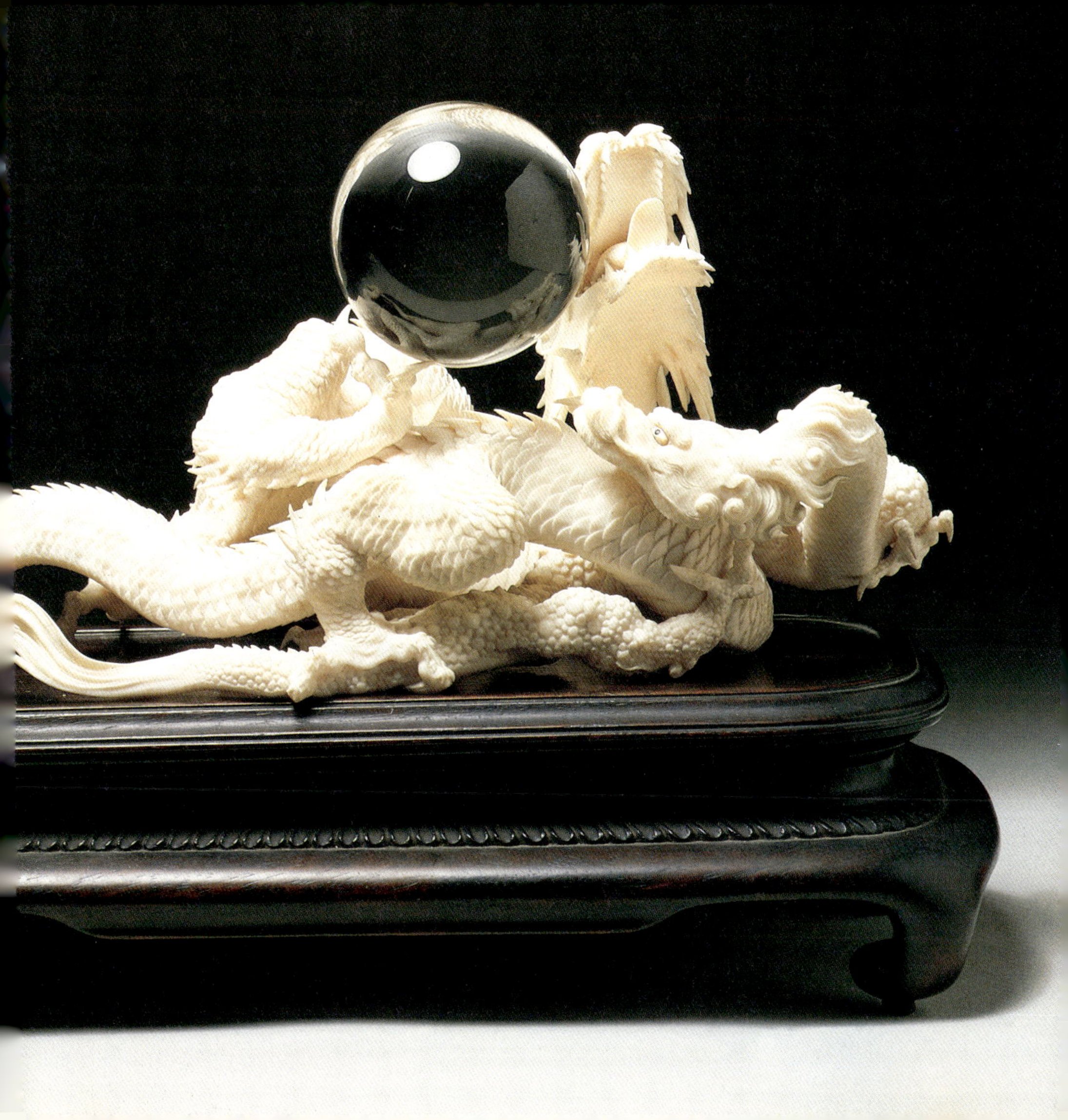

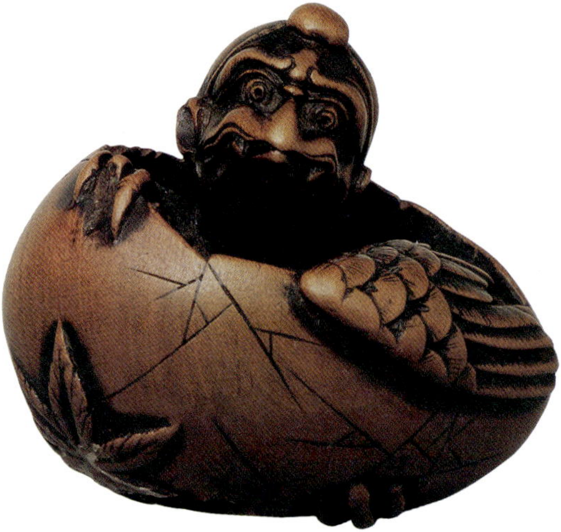

NETSUKE OF WOOD CARVED TO

SHOW A BIRD-HEADED

TENGU HATCHING FROM ITS EGG.

JAPANESE, 18TH CENTURY.

HEIGHT 43MM. A909–1910

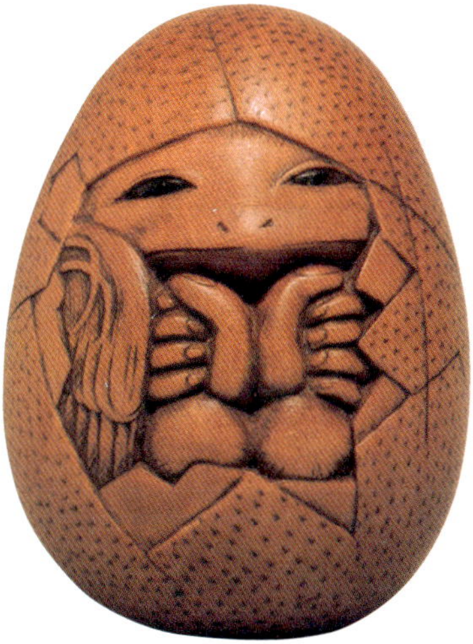

BOXWOOD NETSUKE DEPICTING

A BIRD-HEADED

TENGU HATCHING FROM ITS EGG.

JAPANESE, 19TH

CENTURY. HEIGHT 38MM.

A907–1910

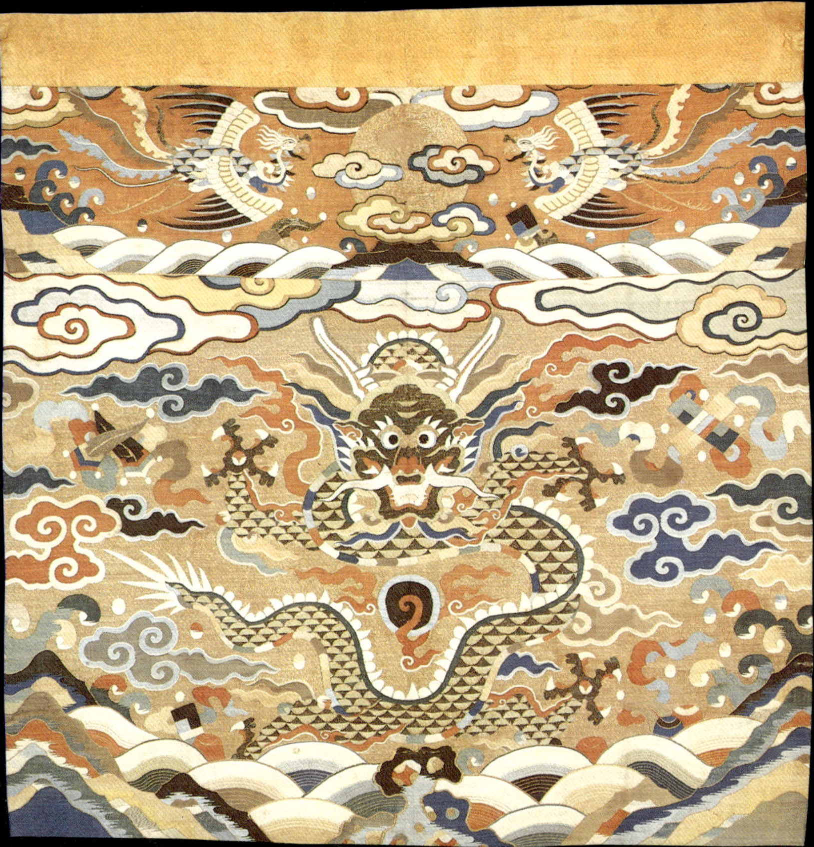

ALTAR FRONTAL

WOVEN IN COLOURED SILKS,

GOLD THREAD AND

PEACOCK FEATHERS. CHINESE,

LATE 16TH CENTURY.

HEIGHT 902MM. FE37–1972

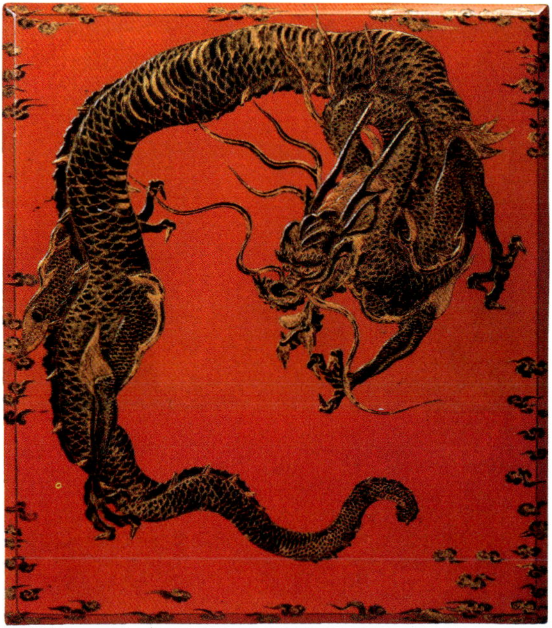

WRITING BOX OF RED LACQUER,

THE LID DECORATED

WITH A DRAGON AND CLOUDS

IN GOLD LACQUER ON

BLACK. JAPANESE, 1626.

197×218MM. W2–1917

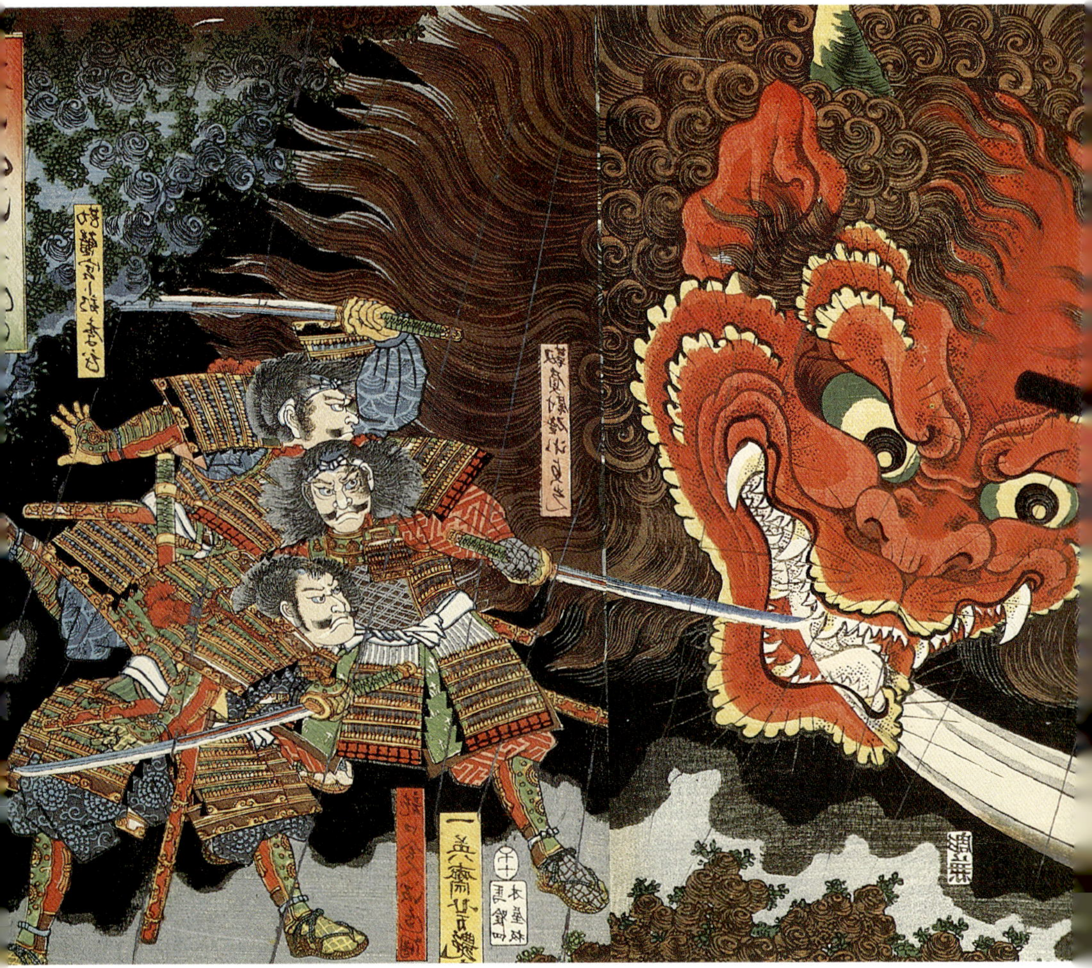

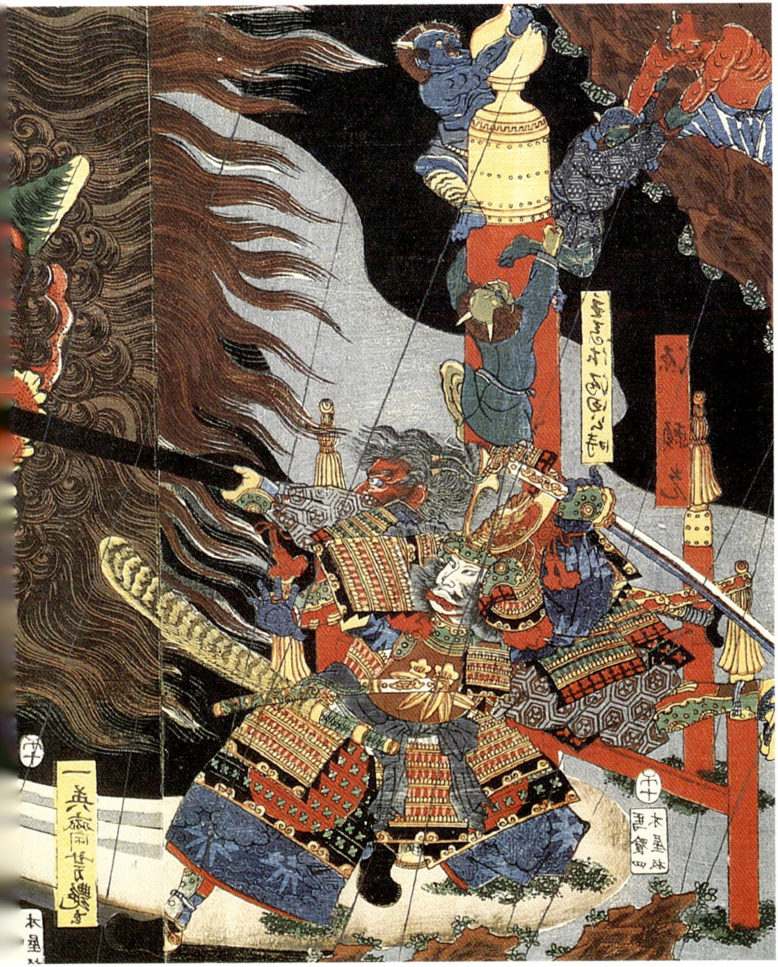

RAIKO AND HIS RETAINERS SLAYING THE OGRE SHUTENDOJI. 1858. UTAGAWA YOSHITSUYA (1822–1866). COLOUR PRINT FROM WOOD BLOCKS. 357×739MM. E14254–1886

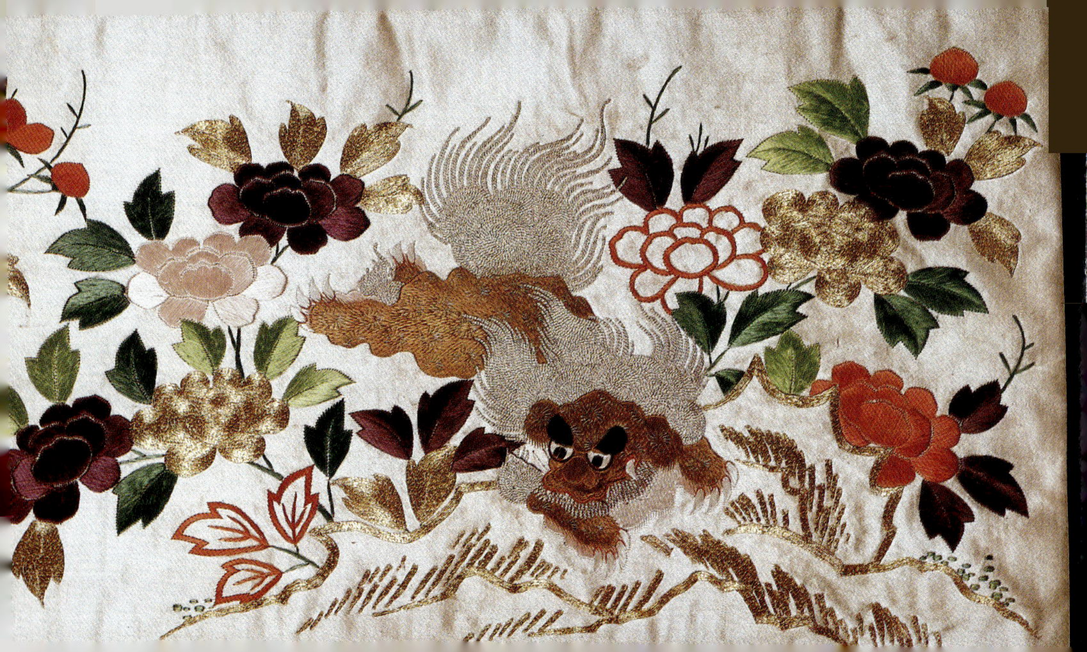

KIMONO SASH (OBI) OF

SATIN EMBROIDERED IN SILK.

JAPANESE, LATE 19TH

CENTURY. 2477×254MM.

T270–1960

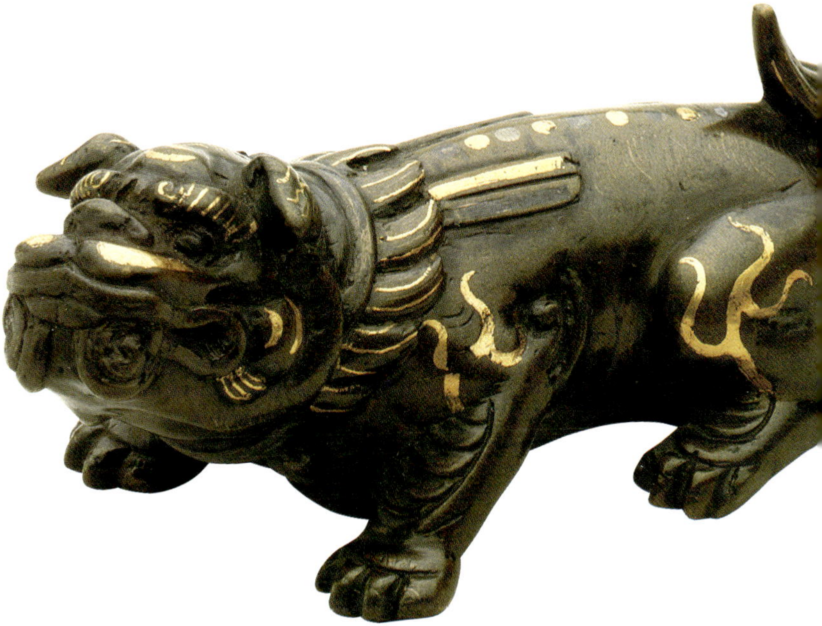

MYTHICAL ANIMAL OF

BRONZE, INLAID WITH GOLD

AND SILVER. CHINESE,

MING DYNASTY. LENGTH 90MM.

FE182–1879

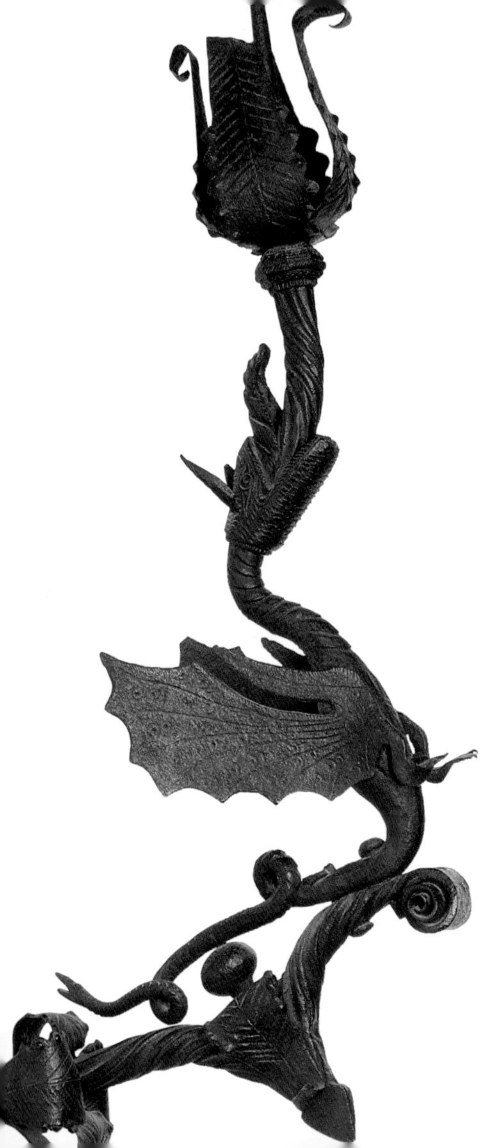

IRON LAMP-BRACKET

ITALIAN, MID 17TH CENTURY.

LENGTH 475MM. M2–1864.

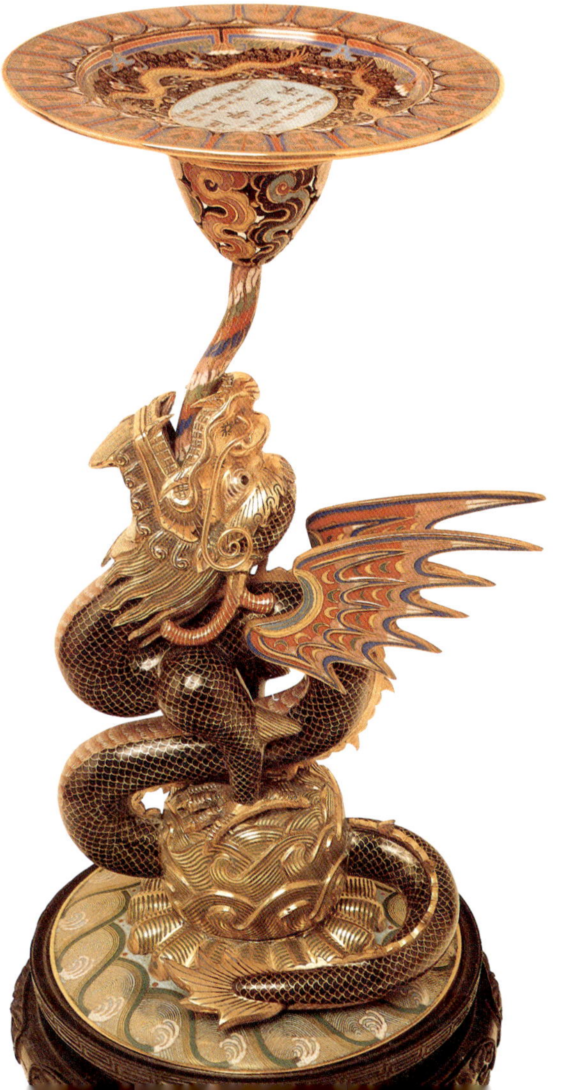

DISH ON A STAND. CLOISONNE ENAMEL ON COPPER GILT. CHINESE (PEKING) 1904. 450MM HIGH. M3–1965

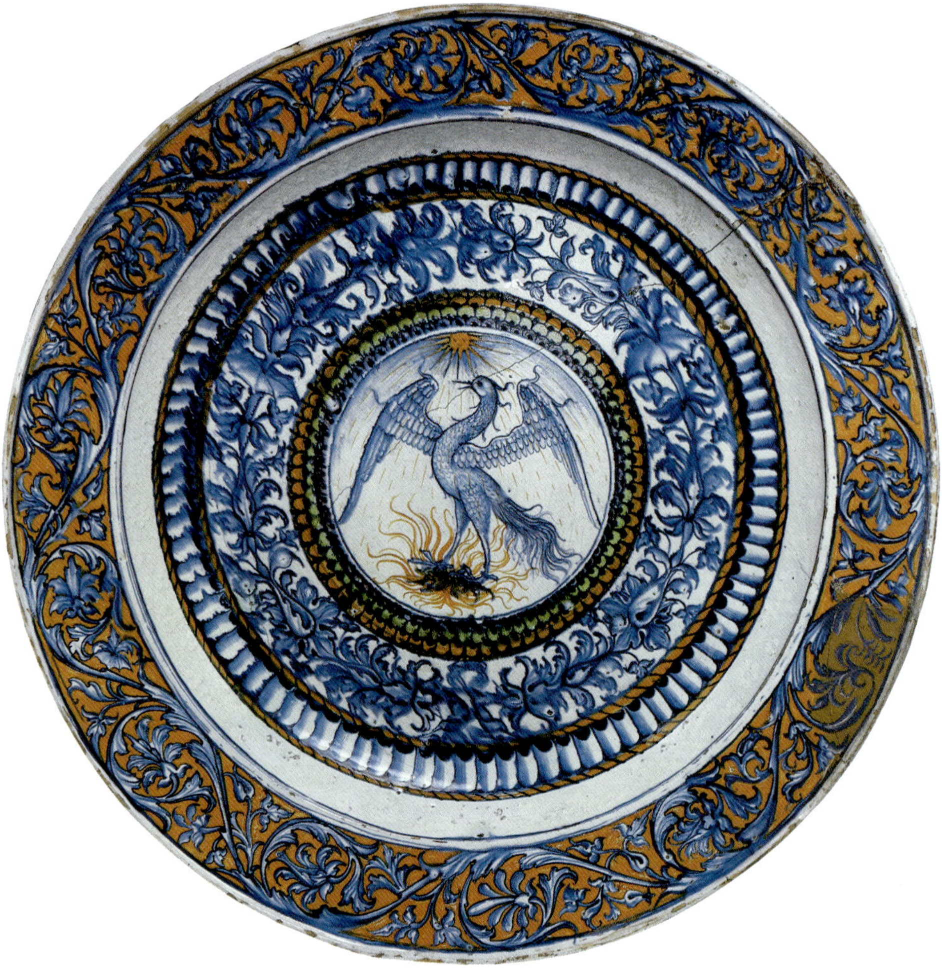

MAIOLICA DISH

DECORATED WITH A PHOENIX.

ITALIAN, *C.* 1530.

DIAMETER 553MM. C651–1884

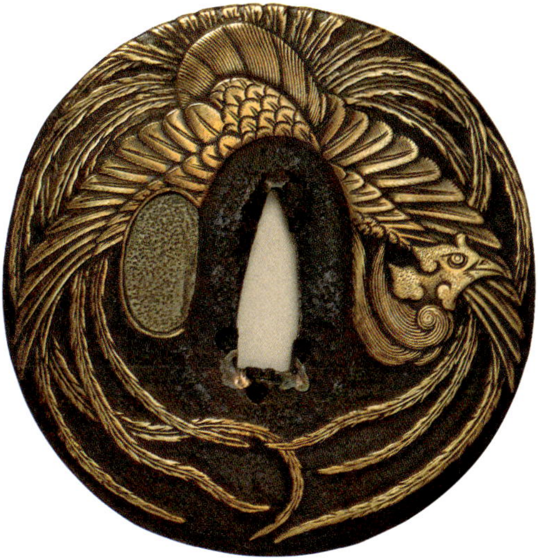

SWORD-GUARD (TSUBA)

OF IRON INLAID WITH BRASS.

JAPANESE. LATE 16TH, EARLY 17TH

CENTURY. 79MM WIDE.

M358–1940

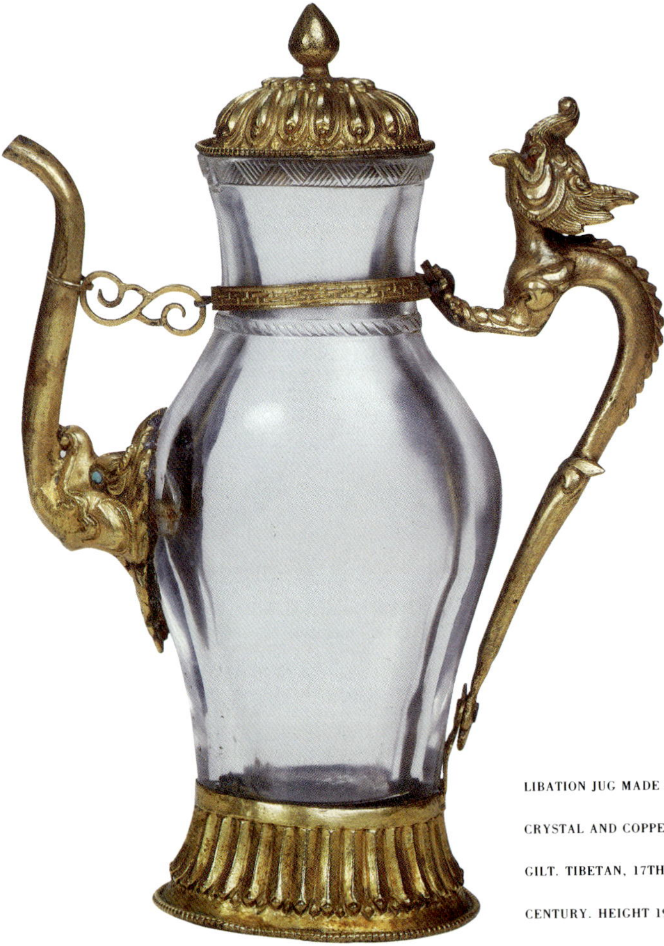

GLASS DECANTER, MOUNTED IN SILVER WHICH HAS BEEN CHASED AND SET WITH SEMI-PRECIOUS STONES AND ROMAN COINS. ENGLISH, DESIGNED BY WILLIAM BURGES, 1865. HEIGHT 279MM. C857–1956

LIBATION JUG MADE FROM ROCK CRYSTAL AND COPPER GILT. TIBETAN, 17TH TO 18TH CENTURY. HEIGHT 192MM. IM379–1914

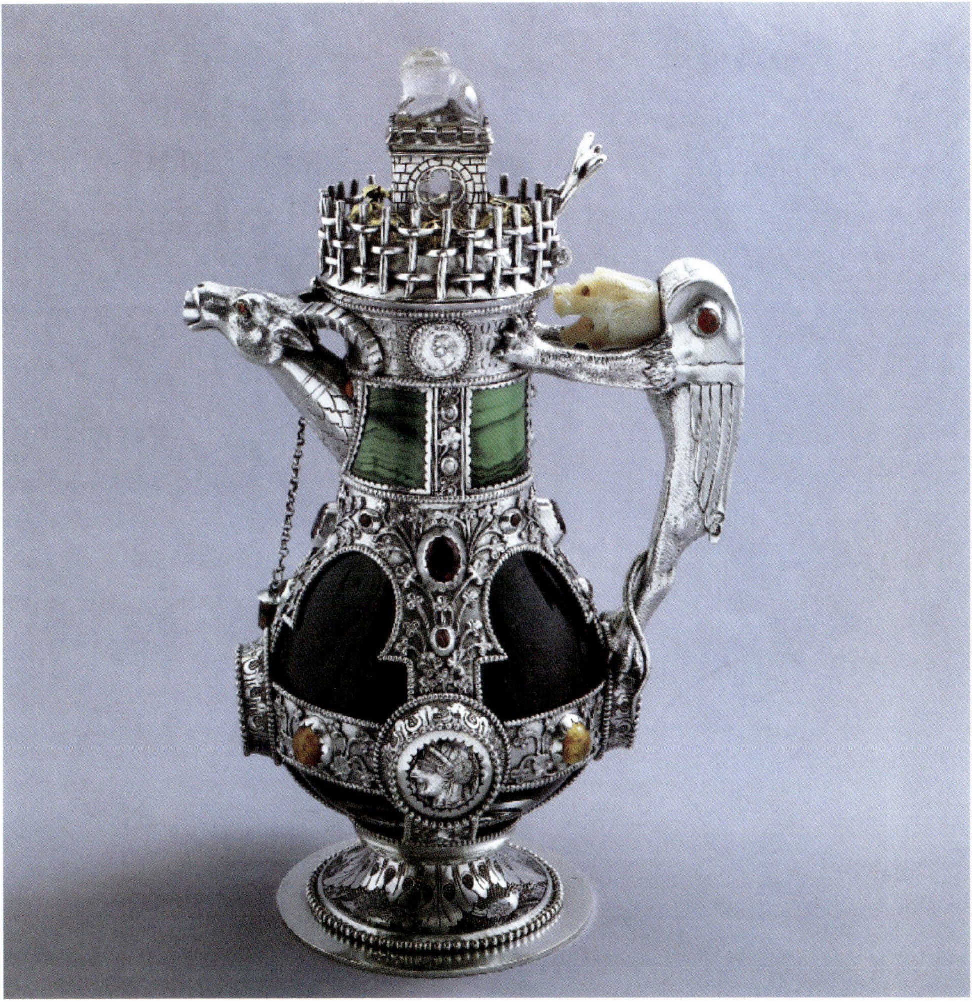

PANEL, PIERCED, EMBOSSED AND PAINTED IRON. SPANISH, FIRST HALF OF THE 16TH CENTURY. HEIGHT 222MM. M429–1927

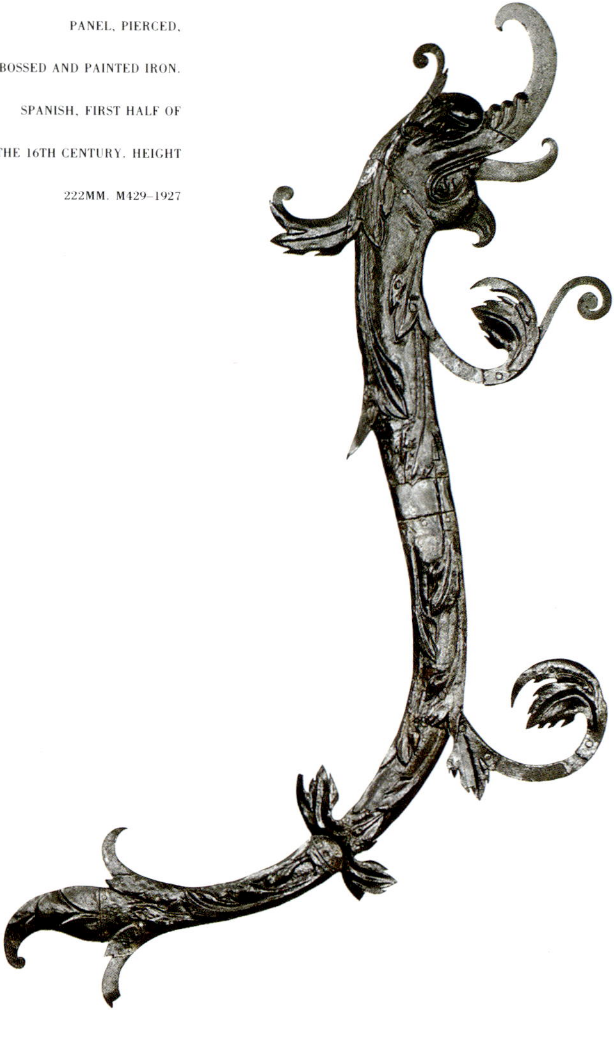

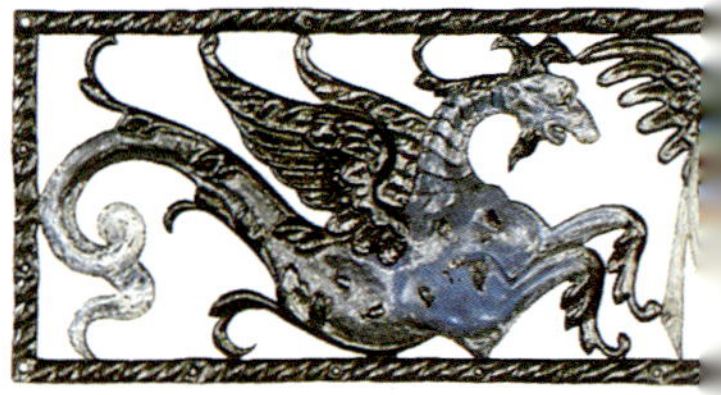

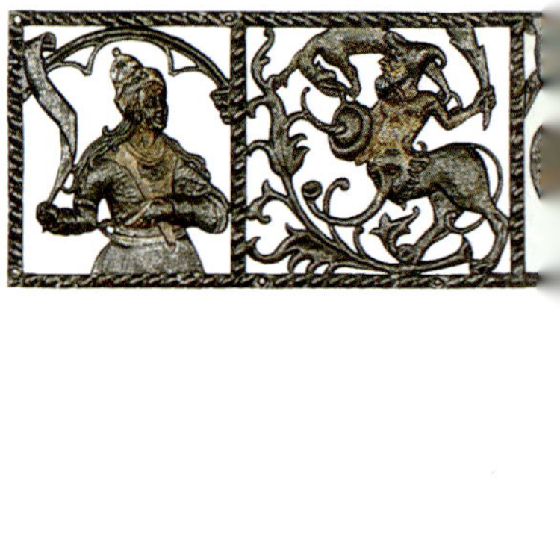

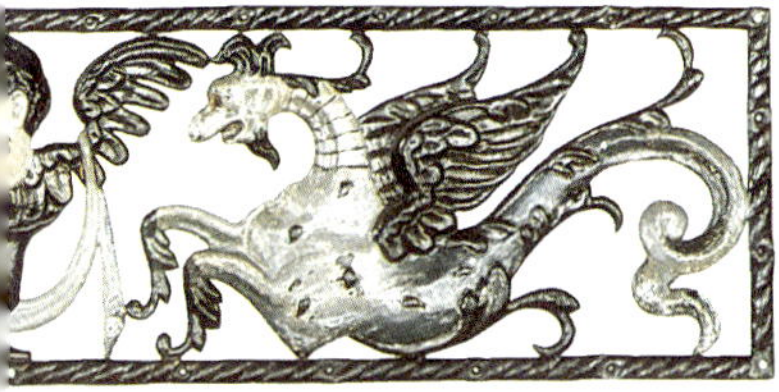

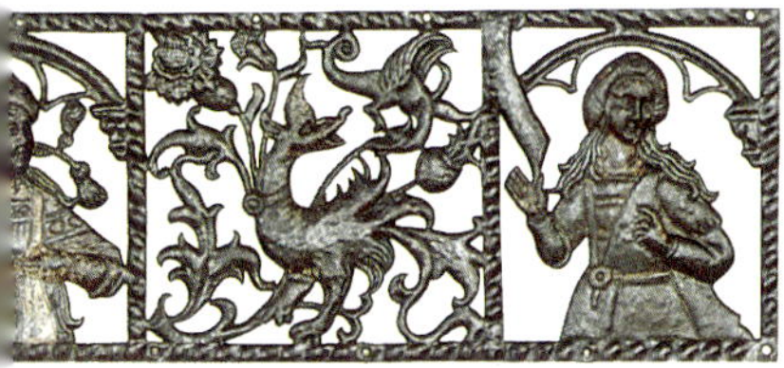

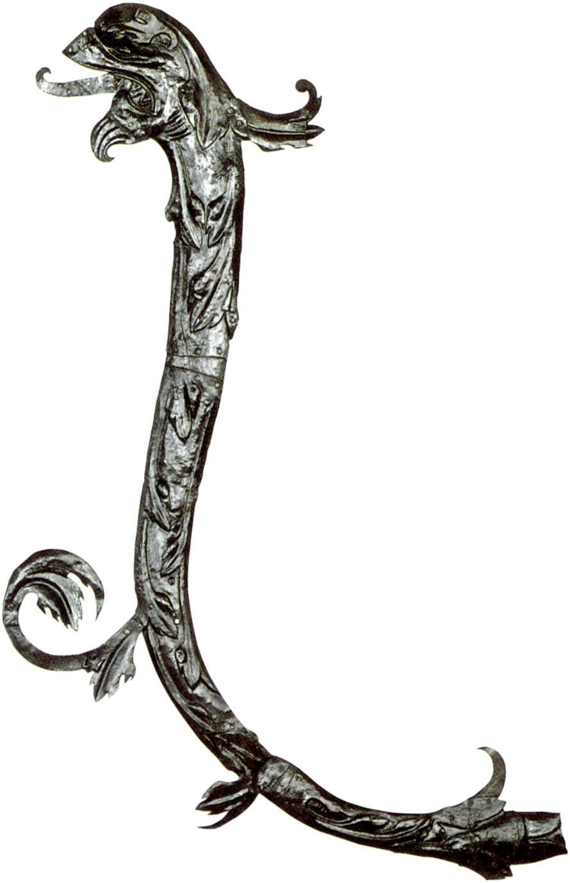

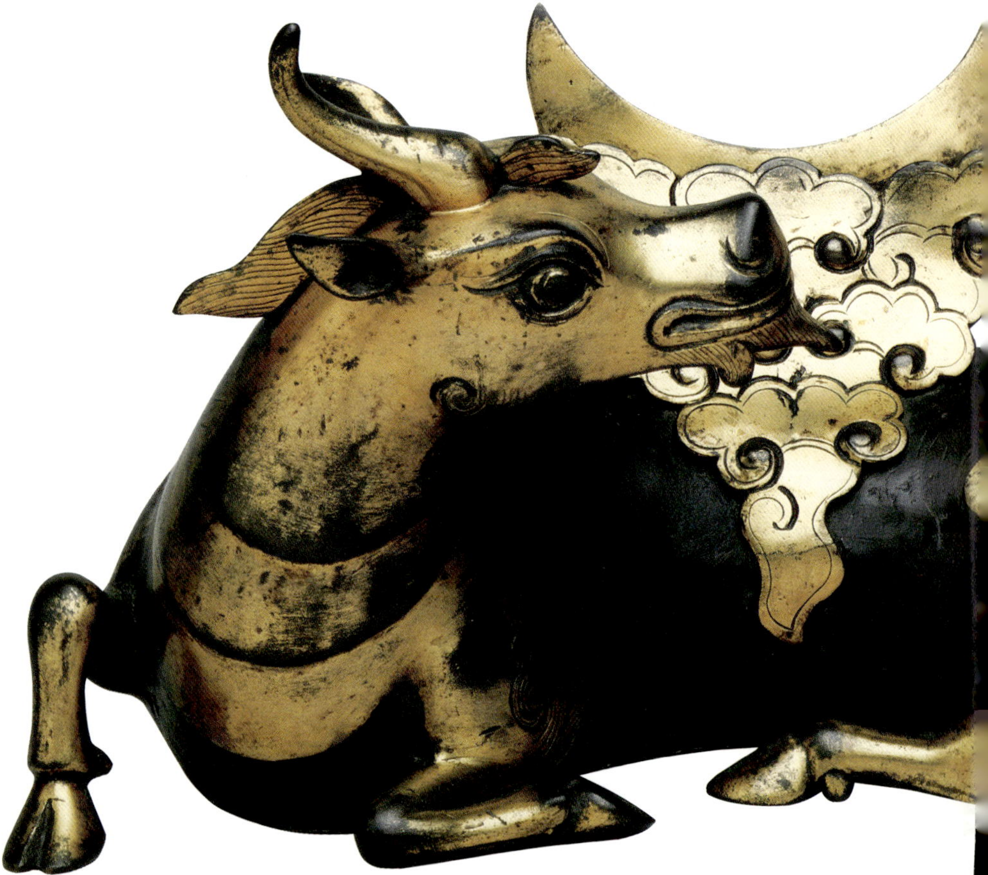

IVORY NETSUKE CARVED WITH

A WINGED HORSE.

JAPANESE, 19TH CENTURY.

41MM. A52–1920

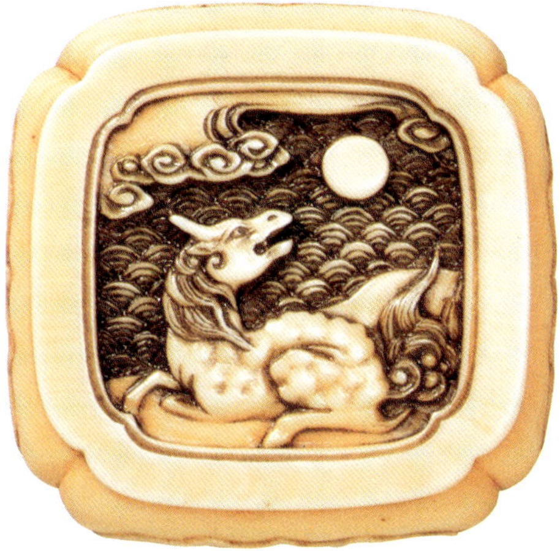

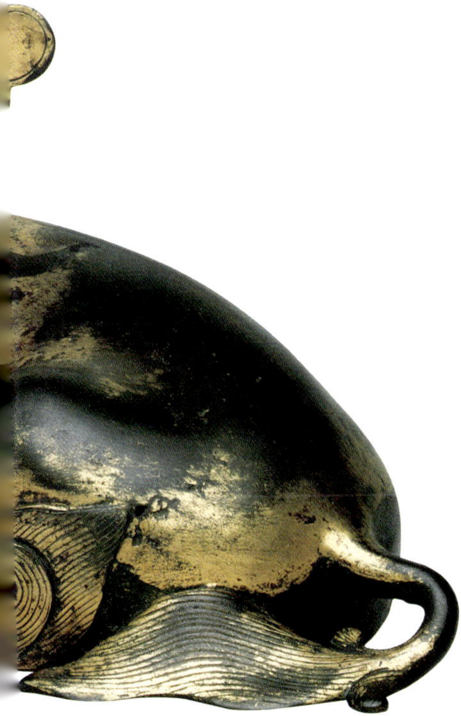

MIRROR STAND OF BRONZE AND

GILT IN THE FORM OF A

UNICORN. CHINESE, SONG-YUAN

DYNASTIES. LENGTH 270MM.

FE737–1910

ENAMELLED PORCELAIN

LION-DOG. JAPANESE, 1670–85.

HEIGHT 120MM. FEC35–1958

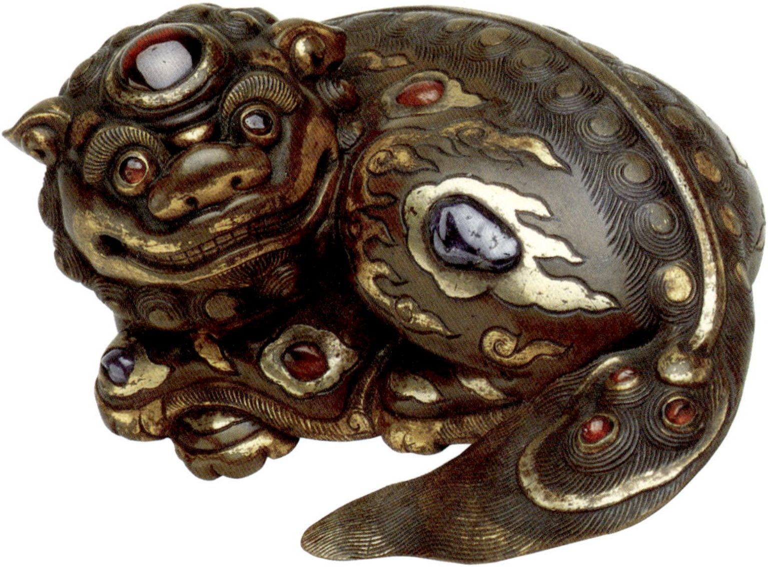

BRONZE MYTHICAL ANIMAL

INLAID WITH GOLD,

SILVER AND SEMI-PRECIOUS

STONES. CHINESE,

MING DYNASTY (1368–1644).

LENGTH 90MM. M741–1910

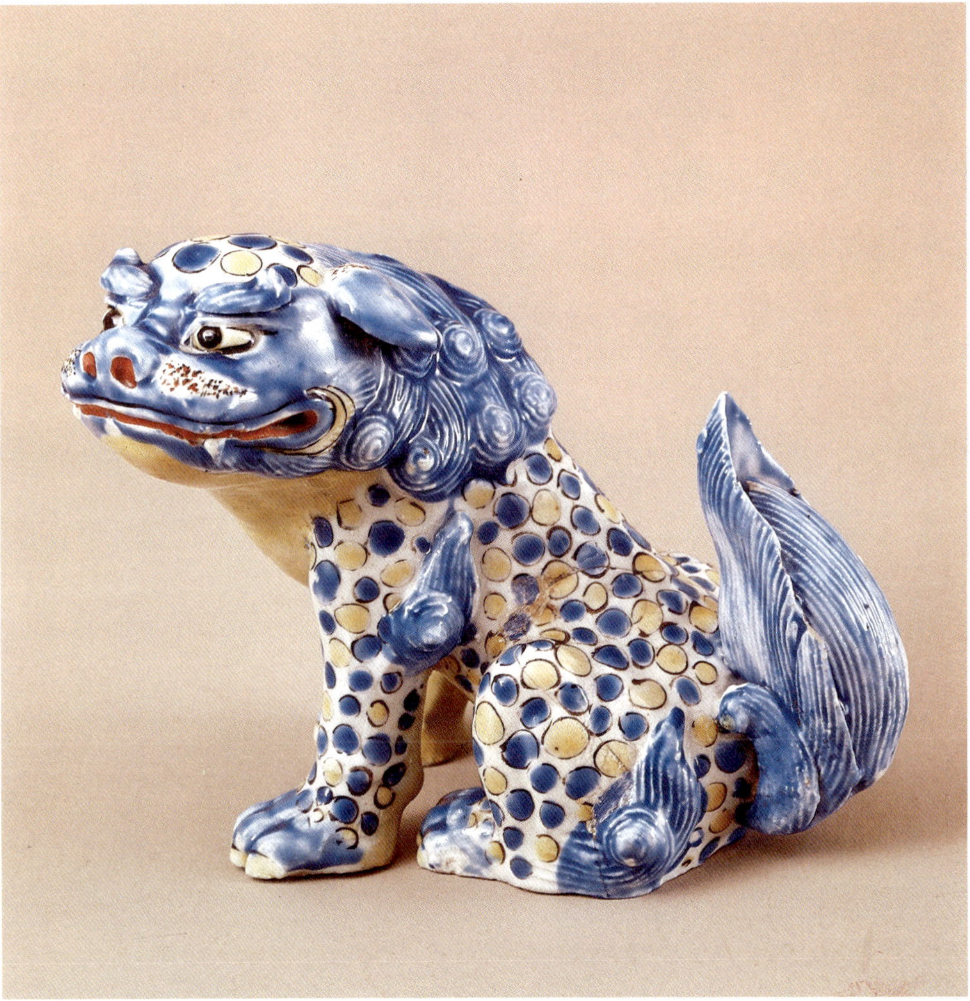

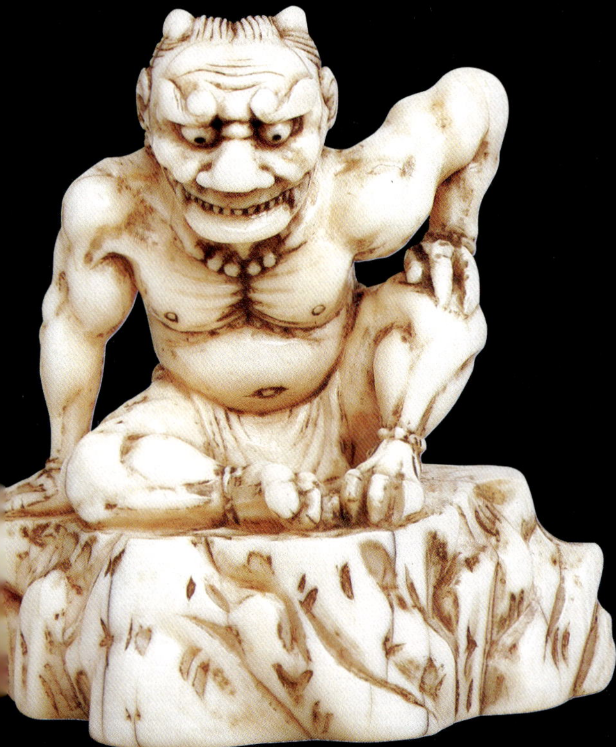

NETSUKE OF IVORY

REPRESENTING A DEMON ON

A ROCK. JAPANESE,

LATE 18TH CENTURY. 41MM.

A459–1904

WOODEN NETSUKE IN THE

FORM OF RAIDEN THE

THUNDER GOD. JAPANESE, 18TH

CENTURY. 51MM. A48–1952

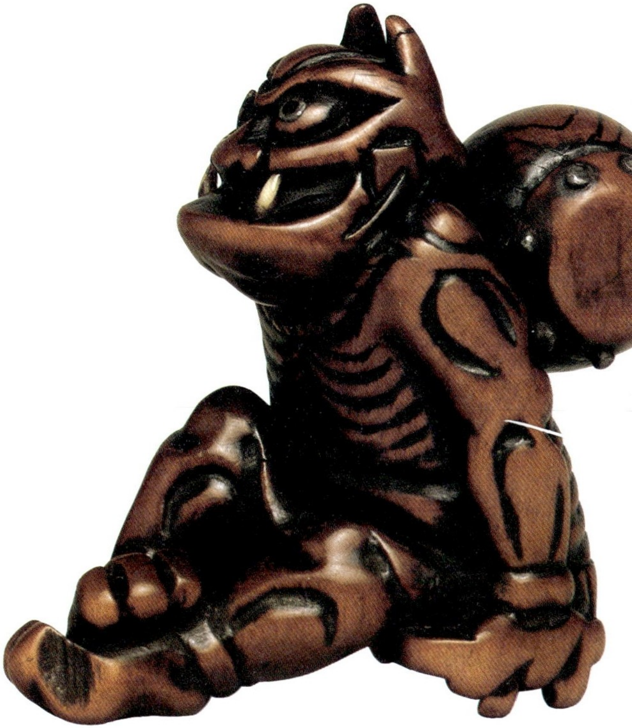

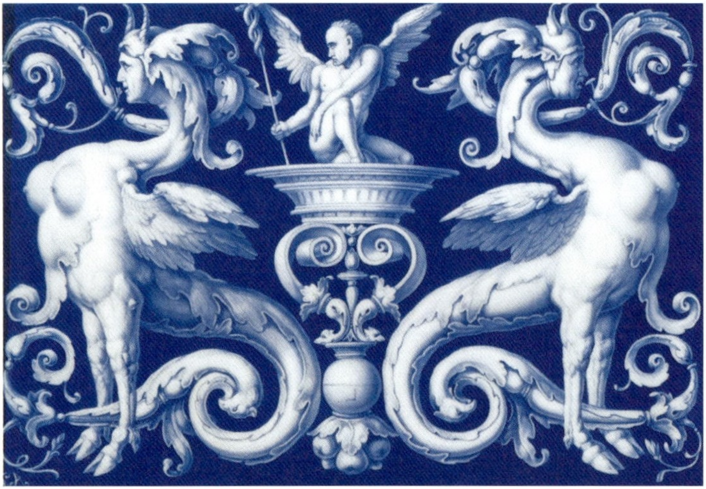

MAIOLICA PLATE

DECORATED WITH A SCENE OF

PERSEUS AND ANDROMEDA.

ITALIAN, *C.* 1520. DIAMETER 270MM.

C2227–1910

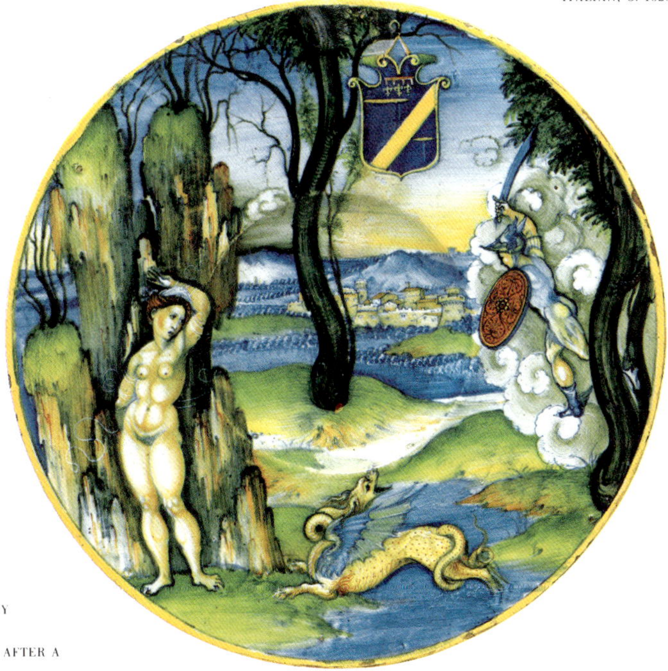

PORCELAIN PANEL BY

ALEXANDER FISHER AFTER A

DESIGN BY LUCAS VAN

LEYDEN, *C.* 1490–1533. PAINTED

IN 1865. ENGLISH.

250×155MM. 171–1866

HEAD OF A TAU

CROSS MADE OF WALRUS IVORY.

ENGLISH, MID 12TH

CENTURY. LENGTH 159MM.

A371–1871

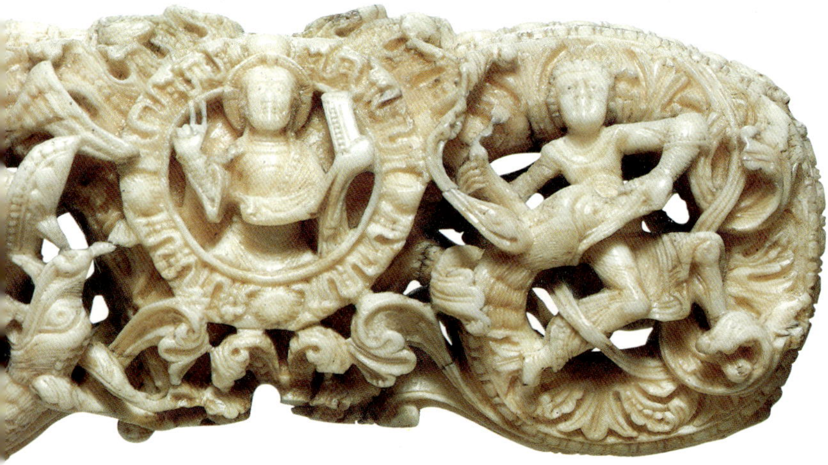

JADE PLAQUE MADE

FOR ATTACHMENT TO CLOTHING.

CHINESE, MING DYNASTY

(1368–1644). DIAMETER 112MM.

FE1643–1882

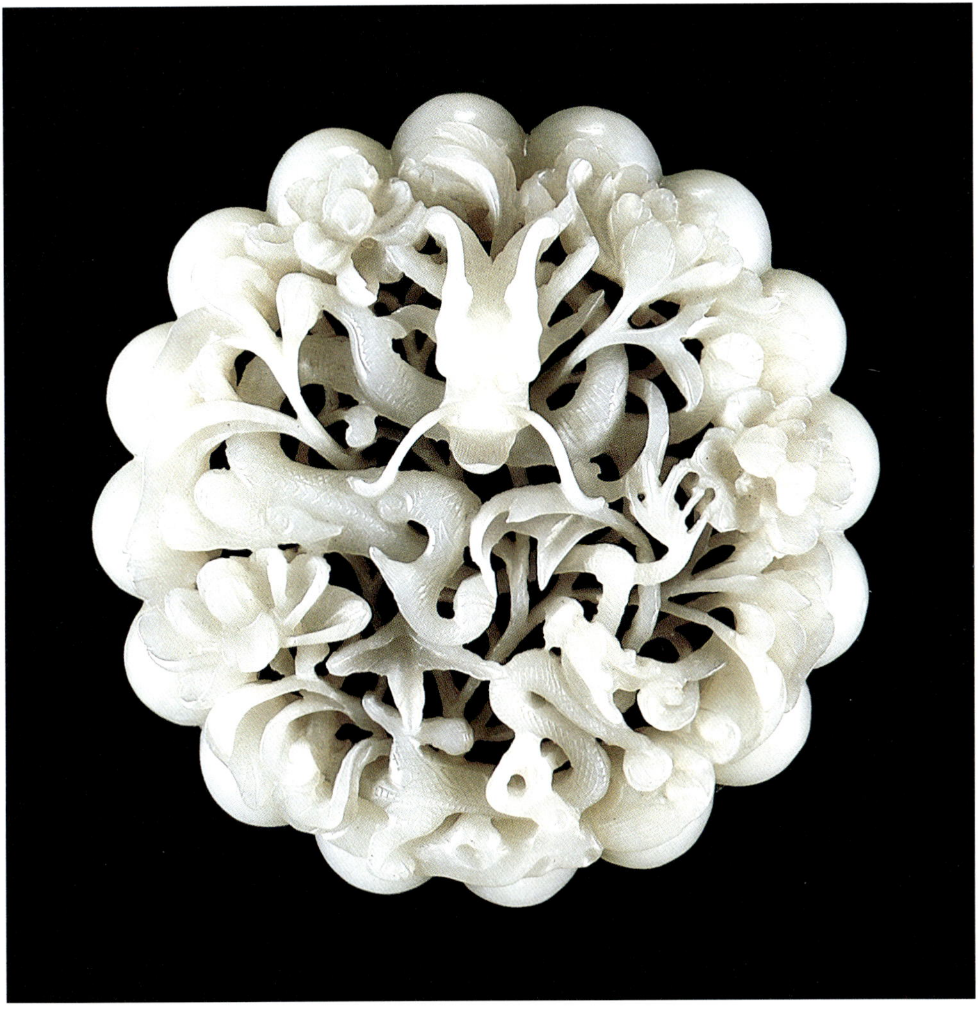

First published in the United States of America, 1992,
by Canopy Books, a division of Abbeville Press, Inc.,
488 Madison Avenue, New York, NY 10022.

First published in Great Britain by the
Victoria and Albert Museum, 1992, Cromwell Road, London.

Printed and bound in Singapore.

ISBN 1-55859-444-2

Series devised by Jennifer Blain and Lesley Burton
Designed by Bernard Higton & Associates
Picture research by Simon Blain